TEXTUAL NOTES

Composition   Mannheim, Nov 1777

Sources   autograph (formerly in Preussische Staatsbibliothek, Berlin) [A]; first edition, as no. 3 of *Trois sonates pour le clavecin ou le forte piano . . . Oeuvre IV* (Paris: Heina, 1782) (nos.1 and 2 are K309/284*b* and K310/300*d*) [E]

Notes   The text basically follows A; where E is the source of an emendation or a possible alternative reading this is noted below, but faults in E, which is inaccurate, are noted only when of possible significance.

CW00644627

Abbreviations in Textual Note
cf. – *confer* [compare]; dsq – dem
K – no. in Köchel catalogue of M
/ is original no., no. after is that in 6th edn, 1904), bar ...
hand; movt – movement; q – quaver; RH – right hand;
sq – semiquaver; stacc. – staccato

Pitch – *c'* is middle C, *d'* the note above, *b* the note below; *c''* and *c'''* one and two octaves above, *c, C* and *C'* one, two and three octaves below

Numerals – arabic numerals in roman normally denote bar nos.; arabic in italic denote note nos. within the bar, counting left to right, chords downwards, and including all grace notes as notated

Editorial notes
In the printing of the text a distinction has been made between original and editorial markings. Slurs and ties added editorially are indicated by a small perpendicular stroke; editorial staccato marks (whether dots or wedges), dynamic markings and accidentals are indicated by the use of smaller type.

Editorial realizations of ornaments are shown in small notes above the text at the first occurrence of the ornament concerned in each movement. These realizations are based on the leading sources contemporary with Mozart, such as C. P. E. Bach's *Versuch über das wahre Art das Clavier zu spielen* (1753–62), Leopold Mozart's *Versuch einer gründlichen Violinschule* (1756) and Daniel Gottlob Türk's *Clavierschule* (1789). Our suggestions should not be taken as mandatory; any proper realization must take account of the tempo chosen for the movement concerned and the player's capabilities, and in a trill a player should feel free to play more notes, or fewer, as seems right. No ornament that feels awkward to the player, or sounds clumsy, is being satisfactorily realized. A player who wants to vary the realization of ornaments more extensively, however, would be well advised first to consult the writings of contemporary authorities, or failing that a summary of their views in a good modern reference work; he should note that except in very rare circumstances a trill should begin on the upper note in music of this period.

1st movt   E: 'Allegro con spiritoso'

bar	
19,81	stacc. from E
20	E, RH, *1–3* slurred, *4–7* stacc.
29	E, RH, *1–3* slurred, *4–9* stacc.
33	E, RH, slurs *1–6, 7–8, 9–10*
35	slurs from E
41	E lacks ♮
96	E, RH, slurs *1–4, 7–10*
106	E, RH, slur from *6* to 107, *1*
110	E has *b''* in 2nd chord

2nd movt

bar	
7	A, slur originally *3–5, 3–6* slur heavily written above; E ambiguous
10	E, RH *1 b'*
11	E, RH *5 e'*; L, LH 2nd slur missing
28	A, LH, *1* slur; cf. 64
29–30, 33–4	A, LH slurs across 2 qs: cf. 65ff
39	E, LH *3 g*; also 75
45	A, RH slur possibly only last 3 sqs
56	A, LH slur *5–8*: cf. 20

3rd movt   Many inconsistencies in articulation in A (and the inaccurate E provides no clarification). For example, the slur on the first two notes and at similar passages, and the staccato on the first LH quavers, are added on the basis of only very few appearances. Mozart rarely marked staccato the first quaver of a triplet when prefixed by an acciaccatura, and this seems deliberate enough to justify deletion of his dots in 176, 249 and 251.

bar	
16–17	slurs in E cover only first 2 notes of each group (also 102–3, 154–5, 256–7)
23	tie from E
58,60	difference in placing of *p* seems intentional: cf. 223, 225 (also in 64–71, 229–36, but these passages are not written out)
159	E lacks turn; A lacks slur, *5–6*
184	A, RH *6 c'♯*
214	A, RH 2nd dot missing

SONATA in D

Allegro con spirito

K311/284c (1777)

MOZART

Sonata in D

for piano

K. 311

Edited by

STANLEY SADIE

Fingering and performance notes by

Denis Matthews

SONATA in D, K311/284c

The original Köchel numbers are misleading here, as the three piano sonatas K309–11 cannot be considered as a group. K310, the remarkable A minor Sonata, was written in Paris in 1778; K309 and K311 were composed, or at least completed, at Mannheim in November or December of the previous year. In fact the D major, K311, may have been begun in Munich that autumn, and it is probably the sonata Mozart referred to as 'still not ready' in a letter to his cousin on 3 December 1777. His travels that winter brought two important influences on his keyboard writing, one direct, one indirect. In Augsburg, *en route* for Mannheim, he played on Stein's improved fortepianos; and in Mannheim he heard one of the finest orchestras in Europe. His next symphony, the 'Paris', was consciously brilliant, and it was in D major, a resonant open-string key for the orchestra. Such key-associations affect other mediums too. His earlier D major Sonata, the so-called 'Dürnitz' Sonata K284, began with a resolute, crisp, 'orchestral' theme, and its first movement has other points in common with the present work, K311 – the lead into, and the start of, the second group, for example.

1 The opening of K311 not only calls for a keen sense of orchestral colour, a tutti chord followed by oboes and horns, but shows the influence of the concerto form too. The events in bb.1–16 closely resemble those in the first movement of the E♭ Piano Concerto, K271 – the astonishingly mature 'early' E♭, written in Salzburg in January 1777, in which the soloist makes a prompt riposte to the orchestra's very first phrase. There is something of this spirited antiphony in K311, whether one regards the first beat of b.4 as an ending or, as in the concerto, an overlap. In the latter case, it is the left hand, not the right, that marks the re-entry of the tutti. Contrast in character should not, however, forestall the first real *piano* in b.7, but the subsequent alternations of *piano* and *forte* continue to suggest the concertante element. Note that the right hand takes the initiative in bb.11, 24, and 66: the left-hand *fortes* come later, a point omitted in some editions, though not of course at the end of b.86, where the major key is triumphantly restored after the unexpected turn to D minor. Although not indicated, the right hand should cross over for the quaver figure in b.27 (compare b.90). Avoid the common fault of attacking the second crotchet of b.30 and elsewhere with a sudden accent: it is the whole phrase that is *forte*, and it should match the previous *piano* one. This feature is delightfully reversed in bb.58–65. Other points to notice are the development's concern with, and sudden abandonment of, the sighing cadence-figure of bb.38–39; and the bypassing of the first subject in the recapitulation. It reappears at b.99, and it may have been the lengthy D major-ness of this section that led Mozart to substitute an interrupted cadence for the expected full close in b.110. The mark 'con spirito' implies a lively crotchet pulse, perhaps a shade livelier than in the first movement of *Eine kleine Nachtmusik*. Nevertheless the semiquavers in bb.13–14 and from b.66 onwards should be just about manageable by a good coloratura. The left-hand slurs in bb.18 and 80 are inconsistent but harmless.

2 Some commentators have remarked on the unusual phrase-lengths of the opening theme, but the eleven repeated bars are in fact incomplete without the twelfth. The unusual feature here is the overlap in b.8, where the treble G both completes the cadence and forms the upbeat of the 'codetta', as the left-hand figure proves. The movement is an object-lesson in discreet embellishment, for each return of the opening brings some new variant. Bar 25, which recalls the first theme within the world of the second, is a Haydnish move. The expressive sequences from b.29, which seem new, derive from b.3. In b.33 Mozart adds trills, and players who begin on the main note can point to the legato slur and the fact that the upper note has already been sounded; but the upper note will enhance the dissonance. Compare the dissonances in bb.23 and 59. Note the reversed dynamics in bb.33–35, and especially from b.69, where the different register allowed Mozart a sudden change of octave: this is an inspiration, not a makeshift, and out of it the further inspiration of bb.72–73 is born. The deep bass crotchets eight bars from the end must obviously be held with pedal, but many early fortepianos had knee-levers which controlled bass and treble dampers independently; on the modern piano the blurring of the right-hand octaves is tolerable, because short-lived, but the sound must be carefully nursed.

3 A sprightly and fully-developed sonata-rondo in 6/8 time, with plenty of brilliant semiquavers and a written-out cadenza (b.173: more strictly a 'lead-in'), inevitably suggests a concerto finale. In that case this particular movement is a forerunner of a type Mozart had yet to adopt in his later piano concertos (K450, K456, K482, K595) and in the so-called 'hunting' finales of the horn concertos. Aubyn Raymar, in the previous Associated Board edition, called for 'grace and lightness'; but there is a masculine robustness in the tambour effects of b.27 and the wide violinistic leaps of b.56. Pianists will benefit, in this last theme, from listening to a good performance of the finale of Mozart's A major Symphony, K201. The middle episode (b.119) follows a favourite plan of Mozart's in introducing a minor-key theme and turning it aside for a carefree one in the subdominant major (see the rondo of the A major concerto, K488). In the first episode and its later reprise, the different placing of the *piano* in bb.58 and 60 is intentional, adding variety and humour to an otherwise straight repetition.

D.M.

© 1971 by The Associated Board of the Royal Schools of Music
Published by ABRSM (Publishing) Ltd, a wholly owned subsidiary of ABRSM

Andante con espressione

RONDEAU
Allegro

RONDEAU
Allegro

Mozart: piano music published by ABRSM

Sonatas

Complete editions

Volume I
paper and cloth editions available
Sonatas, K. 279–284, K. 309–311

Volume II
paper and cloth editions available
Sonatas, K. 330–333, K. 475/457, K. 533, K. 545, K. 570, K. 576

Separate editions

Sonata in F, K. 280
Sonata in B flat, K. 281
Sonata in E flat, K. 282
Sonata in G, K. 283
Sonata in D, K. 284
Sonata in C, K. 309
Sonata in A minor, K. 310
Sonata in D, K. 311
Sonata in C, K. 330
Sonata in A, K. 331
Sonata in F, K. 332
Sonata in B flat, K. 333
Fantasy and Sonata in C minor, K. 475/457
Sonata in C, K. 545
Sonata in F, K. 533
Sonata in B flat, K. 570
Sonata in D, K. 576

Other works

Mature Piano Pieces
  Four Contredanses, K. 269b
  Four Praeambula, K. 284a
  Allegro in B flat, K. 400/372a
  Prelude and Fugue in C, K. 394/383a
  March in C, K. 408 No. 1/383e
  Fantasia in C minor, K. 396/385f
  Fantasia in D minor, K. 397/385g
  Suite in C, K. 399/385i
  Funeral March in C minor, K. 453a
  Rondo in D, K. 485
  Rondo in A minor, K. 511
  Adagio in B minor, K. 540
  Gigue in G, K. 574
  Minuet in D, K. 355/576b
  Andantino in E flat, K. 236/588b
  Allegro in G minor, K. 312/590d
  Andante in F, K. 616
  Adagio in C, K. 356/617a

Nine Variations on a Minuet by J.-P. Duport, K. 573

Fantasia in D minor, K. 397/385g

Rondo in D, K. 485

Rondo in A minor, K. 511

ABRSM
24 Portland Place
London W1B 1LU
United Kingdom

www.abrsm.org

ISBN 978-1-85472-107-5

9 781854 721075